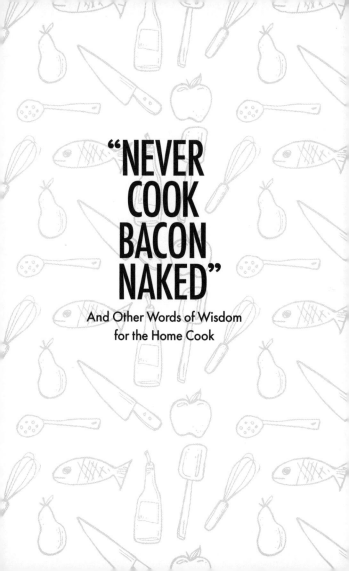

"NEVER COOK BACON NAKED"

And Other Words of Wisdom for the Home Cook

Library of Congress Cataloging-in-Publication Data available upon request.

ISBN: 978-1-947458-21-5

Illustration and design by Kelley Lanuto, Kalanuto Design

duopress books are available at special discounts when purchased in bulk for sales promotions as well as for fund-raising or educational use. Special editions can be created to specification.
Contact us at hello@duopressbooks.com for more information.

Every effort has been made to trace the original quotes that appear in this book. The publisher apologizes for any errors or omissions and would be grateful if notified of any corrections that should be incorporated in future reprints or editions of this book.

Manufactured in China
10 9 8 7 6 5 4 3 2

Duopress LLC
8 Market Place, Suite 300
Baltimore, MD 21202

Distributed by Workman Publishing Company, Inc.
Published simultaneously in Canada by Thomas Allen & Son Limited.

To order: hello@duopressbooks.com
www.punchlineideas.com
www.duopressbooks.com
www.workman.com

"NEVER COOK BACON NAKED"

And Other Words of Wisdom for the Home Cook

Compiled by Doreen Chila-Jones

APERITIF

The title of this book comes from a wedding advice card. As the story goes, artist Jason A. Cina heard the quote from a friend who attended the event. In the note, circa 2005, the couple requested that guests offer their "Special Wishes or Advice for the Newlyweds." The advice was not a brainy and well-intended marriage recommendation, such as "Never disrespect your partner" or "Never go to bed angry." Those tips would have made too much sense. Jason's friend decided to write, "Don't Fry Bacon Naked." Wise.

Years later, Doreen Chila-Jones was busy gathering quotes for this book and contacted her friends for assistance. When Jason sent her his quote, his memory betrayed him and he mistakenly wrote "cook" instead of "fry." The innocent slipup wasn't discovered until a few weeks later, but by then we had all fallen in love with the title of this book and decided to leave it that way. That's the beauty of quotes; they are there to inspire and to teach, not to follow to the letter. After all, who cares if you are "frying" or "cooking" bacon? If you are cooking naked, the technique is the least of your problems. Remember that when you read this book. The goal, after all, is to get inspired and to put some food on the table.

—the punchline team

Jason A. Cina is a painter living in Queens, New York, with his wife, Clarice, and daughter, Juliet. His artwork can be seen at jasonacina.com.

BE CREATIVE

"Cooking is like painting or writing a song. Just as there are only so many colors, there are only so many flavors— It's how you combine them that sets you apart."

—Wolfgang Puck
Austrian-American chef and restaurateur

PUT YOUR HOPES ON IT

"I think that you've got to make something that pleases you and hope that other people feel the same way."

—Thomas Keller

American chef, restaurateur, and cookbook writer

MAKE A PRETTY MEAL

"The keynote to happiness within the four walls that make any home is plain, wholesome, well cooked food, attractively served."

—Louis P. De Gouy
Author of The Soup Book

WHACK A CHICKEN

"The best way to execute French cooking is to get good and loaded and whack the hell out of a chicken. Bon appétit."

—Julia Child
American chef, author, and television personality

USE SOME "HELP"

"I cook with wine.
Sometimes I even add it
to my food."

—W.C. Fields
Actor and writer

NOBODY IS PERFECT

"When you acknowledge, as you must, that there is no such thing as perfect food, only the idea of it, then the real purpose of striving toward perfection becomes clear: To make people happy. That's what cooking is all about."

—Thomas Keller
American chef, restaurateur, and author

BURN YOURSELF (JUST A LITTLE, PLEASE)

"I don't think there's any chef that is born great like in music or in sports. You have to burn yourself...Messing up makes you a better chef."

—David Chang
American restaurateur, author, and television personality

COOK WITH GHOSTS

"No one who cooks, cooks alone. Even at her most solitary, a cook in the kitchen is surrounded by generations of cooks past, the advice and menus of cooks present, and the wisdom of cookbook writers."

—Laurie Colwin
American writer

LEAVE YOUR INHIBITIONS OUT OF THE KITCHEN

"Cooking is like love. It should be entered into with complete abandon or not at all."

—Harriet Van Horne
American journalist

BLAME THE RECIPE

"I don't think there
are bad cooks, just
bad recipes."

—Deb Perelman
Writer,
The Smitten
Kitchen Cookbook

"Tis an ill cook that cannot lick his own fingers."

—William Shakespeare
Romeo and Juliet

YES, BUT DON'T OVERPROCESS!

"Become familiar with the techniques you use and the foods you cook. Learn to respond to the process with your senses, and ultimately you will be in control of the process."

—Lidia Matticchio
  Bastianich
  *Cookbook author
  and restaurateur*

THINK ABOUT THIS

"Cooking is at once child's play and adult joy. And cooking done with care is an act of love."

—Craig Claiborne
American restaurant critic and author

OK...I GUESS

"I cook. My favorite thing to make is love."

—Jarod Kintz
Author

OHHHH, TRUMAN

"Oh, I adore to cook. It makes me feel so mindless in a worthwhile way."

—Truman Capote
American novelist, screenwriter, playwright, and actor

DEBATE IS OPTIONAL

"Only a fool argues with a
skunk, a mule, or a cook."

—Old cowboy saying

IT'S JUST COOKING

"If at the end of the day
if nothing is on fire, no
one went to the hospital,
you didn't have to call a
plumber and your feet don't
stick to the floor, it was
a success!"

—Angie Parisi
*Italian cook
and music lover*

LEAVE IT TO
THE FRENCH

"Cooking is not difficult.
Everyone has taste, even if
they don't realize it.
Even if you're not a great
chef, there's nothing to
stop you understanding the
difference between
what tastes good and
what doesn't."

—Gérard Depardieu
*French actor, filmmaker,
businessman, and
vineyard owner*

BE A SUPERHERO

"Your apron is just a cape on backwards."

—Unknown

DO THE OBVIOUS!

"The only way to become
a cook is to cook."

—Julia Turshen
Author of Small Victories

EGGS = SMILES

"All it takes to be a good cook is an egg, a hungry person, and the desire to put a smile on their face."

—Bryan Voltagio
Chef and cookbook author

BE GENEROUS

"Cooking is about creating something delicious for someone else."

—Ayumi Komura
Japanese manga artist

COOK FOR YOUR OWN HEALTH

"Let food be thy medicine and medicine be thy food."

—Hippocrates
Ancient Greek physician

IT'S ALL ABOUT THE INGREDIENTS

"If you keep good food in your fridge, you will eat good food."

—Errick McAdams
Personal trainer

LISTEN TO THE POETS

"I'm just someone who likes cooking and for whom sharing food is a form of expression."

—Maya Angelou
American poet, memoirist, and civil rights activist

SAY WHAT?

"A good cook is like a sorceress who dispenses happiness."

—Elsa Schiaparelli
Italian fashion designer

THINK LIKE A CHINESE PHILOSOPHER

"Govern a great nation as you would cook a small fish. Do not overdo it."

—Lao Tzu
Ancient Chinese philosopher

THE TAO OF PALTROW

"Invest in what's real. Clean as you go. Drink while you cook. Make it fun. It doesn't have to be complicated. It will be what it will be."

—Gwyneth Paltrow
American actress and food writer

EAT, SLEEP, AND BE LOVED

"One cannot think well, love well, and sleep well if one has not dined well."

—Virginia Woolf
English writer

BECAUSE GIFT CARDS ARE OVERRATED

"Cooking is one of the greatest gifts you can give to those you love."

—Ina Garten
*American author
and cooking show host*

KEEP YOUR PHONE CLOSE BY

"Cooking rule: If at first you don't succeed, order pizza."

—Unknown

THINK ABOUT YOUR SPIRIT

"I think preparing food and feeding people brings nourishment not only to our bodies but to our spirits. Feeding people is a way of loving them, in the same way that feeding ourselves is a way of honoring our own creativeness and fragility."

—Shauna Niequist
Author and blogger

NOT YOUR FAULT

"Chefs don't make mistakes;
they invent new dishes."

—Elizabeth Briggs
*Professor at the
Culinary Institute of America*

EXPERIENCE NOT REQUIRED

"We don't need to be professionals to cook well."

—Tamar Adler
Author,
An Everlasting Meal:
Cooking with Economy
and Grace

JUST DO IT

"The only real stumbling block is fear of failure. In cooking you've got to have a WHAT-THE-HELL attitude."

—Julia Child

SIMPLE AND HONEST

"People want honest, flavorful food, not some show-off meal that takes days to prepare."

—Ted Allen
*American author
and television personality*

PERFECTLY IMPERFECT PERFECTION!

"Homemade food is the opposite of perfection."

—Alana Chernila
Author of
The Homemade Kitchen:
Recipes for Cooking
with Pleasure

WELL SAID,
MR. THEROUX!

"Cooking requires confident guesswork and improvisation— experimentation and substitution, dealing with failure and uncertainty in a creative way."

—Paul Theroux
*American travel writer
and novelist*

RESPECT

"Cooking is at once one of the simplest and most gratifying of the arts, but to cook well one must love and respect food."

—Craig Claiborne

BÉCHAMEL, BÉARNAISE, ROUX... SAY WHAT?

"Sauces can often seem daunting and perhaps a little technical—the classic French names themselves can make simple sauces sound far more complicated than they are in reality. But most are easily conquered."

—Clara Paul
 and Eric Trevillé
 *Authors of 200 Skills
 Every Cook Must Have*

ALL YOU NEED IS LOVE

"Cooking is love made edible."

—Unknown

PRACTICE. COMPARE. REPEAT.

"Just like becoming an expert in wine—you learn by drinking it, the best you can afford—you learn about great food by finding the best there is, whether simply or luxurious. Then you savor it, analyze it, and discuss it with your companions, and you compare it with other experiences."

—Julia Child

LISTEN TO
THE MASTERS

"A recipe has no soul.
You as the cook must bring
soul to the recipe."

—Thomas Keller

TRUST

"Instinct, whether on the ground or in the kitchen, is not a destination but a path."

—Tamar Adler

BE SCIENTIFIC

"I approach cooking from a science angle because I need to understand how things work. If I understand the egg, I can scramble it better. It's as simple as that."

—Alton Brown
American television personality, food-show presenter, and author

SHARE YOUR LIFE EXPERIENCE

"For me, cooking is an expression of the land where you are and the culture of that place."

—Wolfgang Puck

NO DUMMIES ALLOWED

"Cooks are in some ways very much like actors; they must be fit and strong, since acting and cooking are two of the most exacting professions. They must be blessed—or cursed, whichever way you care to look at it—with what is called the artistic temperament, which means that if they are to act or cook at all well, it cannot be for duds or dummies."

—Andre L. Simon
A Concise Encyclopedia
of Gastronomy

SWEET AND...SOUR?

"Get in the habit of labeling everything in the kitchen. Otherwise you may end up making some really salty cookies."

—Nathaniel Nguyen
Executive chef,
The Prince & Pantry

WE RECOMMEND NOT TYING UP YOUR FAMILY AND FRIENDS

"I strongly believe that the more time families and friends spend together cooking and eating, the stronger those family ties and friendships will become."

—Emeril Lagasse
American chef, restaurateur, television personality, and cookbook author

BE AN ARTIST

"Cooking is an art, but you eat it too."

—Marcella Hazan
Italian cooking writer

HAPPINESS IS...

"Cooking is simply a huge and often very fun puzzle of piecing together techniques with different ingredients. Once you know your basics, the world is your oyster (or your clam, your chicken thigh, block of tofu— whatever makes you happy)."

—Julia Turshen

EAT, PLEASE

"You have to eat to cook.
You can't be a good cook
and be a non-eater.
I think eating is the secret
to good cooking."

—Julia Child

SO BROOKLYN

"A good meal can be an adventure—a discovery of new tastes that roll around on your tongue and bring all conversation to a halt as you savor the blend of perfection in your mouth. It can also be like coming home—a meal that is familiar and without surprise but offers the comfort and assurance of good conversation and a loving hug."

—Anne Gilman
Brooklyn-based artist

PLAY WITH YOUR FOOD!

"Let the kids play with their food! Make silly food faces, shape bread dough spiders, and have fun together in the kitchen creating art you can eat!"

—Deanna F. Cook
Children's cookbook author,
Baking Class and
Cooking Class

FIND MEANING

"Cooking and shopping for food brings rhythm and meaning to our lives."

—Alice Waters
American chef, restaurateur, activist, and author

BAKE SOME BROWNIES

"Good things come to those who bake."

—Unknown

BAKING IS RELAXING

"[Bread making is] one of those almost hypnotic businesses, like a dance from some ancient ceremony. It leaves you filled with peace, and the house filled with one of the world's sweetest smells...there is no chiropractic treatment, no Yoga exercise, no hour of meditation in a music-throbbing chapel, that will leave you emptier of bad thoughts than this homely ceremony of making bread."

—M.F.K. Fisher
American food writer

LISTEN TO
THE MAESTRO

"I realized very early the power of food to evoke memory, to bring people together, to transport you to other places, and I wanted to be a part of that."

—José Andrés
Spanish-American chef

STICK AROUND

"Glue yourself to any fine cook you meet."

—Jim Harrison
American poet

BE ONE WITH THE FOOD

"Cook in the moment.
Cook the way you are
feeling, cook to suit the
weather, cook with your
mood, or to change
your mood."

—Sean Brock
Author of Heritage

DON'T BE
CAUGHT UNAWARES

"The bottom line is this:
in order to be a good cook,
you have to be aware of
everything around you.
It's an ongoing process,
one you should take pleasure
in. The more pleasure you
take from cooking, the more
fun you have in the kitchen,
the better your food will be!"

—Thomas Keller

ONE IS THE
LONELIEST NUMBER

"I admire the hell out
of people who cook for
themselves...but for me,
unless there is someone to
cook for, friend or stranger,
the pleasure is missing."

—Katie Workman
Cookbook author of
The Mom 100 Cookbook
and Dinner Solved

BE PREPARED!

"Considering the individual components of a recipe and prepping them will save time and energy and stress and change your cooking process for the better."

—Amanda Freitag
Chef and television personality

YEAH, BABY

"You are the boss of that dough!"

—Julia Child

DON'T WASTE FOOD

"The most remarkable thing about my mother is that for thirty years she served the family nothing but leftovers. The original meal has never been found."

—Calvin Trillin
American journalist, humorist, food writer, poet, memoirist, and novelist

NEVER MEASURE

"Cookery is not chemistry. It is an art. It requires instinct and taste rather than exact measurements."

—Marcel Boulestin
French chef, restaurateur, and author

SH*T HAPPENS...
DEAL WITH IT

"Things are going to go wrong. The great chefs are the ones that don't let it fluster them. They just move through it."

—Michael Symon
*Chef and
television personality*

LOCK AND LOAD!

"My weapon of choice is the frying pan."

—Stephen King
Best-selling horror author

DON'T LOAF AROUND, JUST BAKE IT!

"Bread, like so many staples, is one of those foods that we imagine to be more of a project than it really is. In fact, there are dozens of easy ways to make bread at home."

—Alana Chernila

SAGE ADVICE

"Don't drop the knife."

—Rowan Jacobsen
From Yankee Magazine

IS IT GETTING HOT IN HERE?

"Cooking and sex are intrinsically related. Both require preparation, proper equipment, desire and, of course, execution. Having said that, it's easy to burn or get burned."

—David Unger
Author of
The Price of Escape
and The Mastermind

IT'S NOT ROCKET SCIENCE, AFTER ALL

"You don't need a degree in domestic science to be a good cook."

—Linda McCartney
Singer

PRACTICE MAKES PROGRESS!

"Like riding a bike, learning to drive, or making 'beautiful love,' you might not always get things right first time around, but the benefits when you crack it are incredible."

—Jamie Oliver
British chef and activist

SIMPLY SUPER

"Tenderness in baking is usually the result of simple, but superb technique — proper measuring, mixing, and timing. It's easier than you think."

—Alice Medrich
Author of
Chocolate Holidays

ARE YOU CRAFTY?

"No matter how much creativity goes into it, cooking is an art. Or perhaps I should say a craft. It abides by absolute rules, physics, chemistry, etc. and that means that unless you understand the science you cannot reach the art. We're not talking about painting here. Cooking's more like engineering. I happen to think that there is great beauty in great engineering."

—Alton Brown

IT IS REALLY ABOUT LOVE...

"The most indispensable ingredient of all good home cooking: love for those you are cooking for."

—Sophia Loren
Italian film actress

SHARING IS CARING

"If you cook for people you love and teach them to cook for themselves, they will pass it on."

—Lucinda Scala Quinn
*Cookbook author,
Mad Hungry and
Mad Hungry Family*

KEEP IT SIMPLE

"There are many good reasons to stay home and cook. And, even though we may not always have the energy to invest in a complex meal, making one simple, delicious dish (maybe two) is certainly manageable."

—David Tanis
Chef, New York Times food columnist, and author of One Good Dish

TASTE. TASTE. TASTE.

"Whether you're cooking a recipe from a cookbook that you've never tried before, or whipping up your signature classic, it is essential to taste, taste, and taste."

—Cal Peternell
Chef at Chez Panisse,
Berkeley, California

CAN YOU FEEL IT?

"Good food and good cooking are about more than how the food tastes or looks on a plate; they are about how good the food makes the person cooking it and the person eating it feel."

—Floyd Cardoz

Chef and author of Flavorwalla

BE LIKE LANCELOT...

"Only the pure in heart can make a good soup."

—Ludwig van Beethoven
German composer and pianist

REALLY?

"So, I'll just come out and say it—my name is Amanda Freitag, executive chef, and I'm afraid of cooking at home!"

—Amanda Freitag

IT'S A JEKYLL AND HYDE THING

"I watch cooking change the cook, just as it transforms the food."

—Laura Esquivel
Mexican novelist, screenwriter, and politician

PICK YOUR BATTLES...

"The only time to eat diet food is while you're waiting for the steak to cook."

—Julia Child

THIS CALLS FOR SOME ROYAL JELLY

"I think baking cookies is equal to Queen Victoria running an empire. There's no difference in how seriously you take the job, how seriously you approach your whole life."

—Martha Stewart
Businesswoman, writer, and television personality

DON'T FORGET DESSERT

"You can't buy happiness. But you can buy ice cream and that's about the same thing."

—Unknown

DON'T BE A FAKE COOK: IMPROVISE!

"Real cooks don't need a recipe. They can look at their ingredients, consider their options, and make a meal."

—Sara Moulton
American chef, author, and television personality

I OWE YOU BIG TIME!

"Always serve too much hot fudge sauce on hot fudge sundaes. It makes people overjoyed and puts them in your debt."

—Judith Olney
Author, The Joy of Chocolate

EMBRACE INTIMACY...

"Sharing food with another human being is an intimate act that should not be indulged in lightly."

—M.F.K. Fisher

L'CHAIM!

"Pull up a chair. Take a taste. Come join us. Life is so endlessly delicious."

—Ruth Reichl
American chef and food writer

PROVERB WISDOM

"Full belly; Happy heart."

—Mexican proverb

IF MY FOOD SPEAKS OR SINGS, I'M OUTTA' THERE

"Just get the best and freshest ingredients and let them speak, or sing, for themselves. Do not smother them in sauces."

—Sara Moulton

IT'S TRUE...

"There is no sincerer love than the love of food."

—George Bernard Shaw
Irish playwright

BELLY OVER BRAIN

"The belly rules the mind."

—Spanish proverb

BE A CONTROL FREAK!

"Make your own food.
You'll be surprised at what a
difference it makes when you
take control of the ingredients
in your f*cking food."

—Thug Kitchen: Eat Like
You Give a F*ck

SAY NO TO SHORTCUTS

"There's no substitute for time in the kitchen. Cooking cannot be rushed. If the recipe calls for a simmer for 30 minutes, boiling it for 10 is not a good substitute."

—Nathaniel Nguyen

START STRONG

"Done right, the first course
settles us in at the table."

—Cal Peternell

SIZE MATTERS...

"Always start out with a larger pot than what you think you need."

—Julia Child

MUST BE SOMETHING IN THE AIR

"From morning coffee on the back porch to full-fledged picnics in the woods, everything just tastes better outside."

—Alana Chernila

L'AMORE DELLA MADRE

"It is hard to judge if one's own mother was a good cook. Hers is the first food we eat and there is nothing to compare it to, and there is so much love around it."

—Federico Fellini
Italian film director and screenwriter

"Remember, people are coming to your home, not to a restaurant."

—Julia Turshen

REACH FOR THE STARS!

"The discovery of a new dish does more for the happiness of mankind than the discovery of a star."

—Anthelme Brillat-Savarin
French lawyer and politician

LESS IS LESS...OR MORE...MORE OR LESS

"Everything in moderation.
Including moderation."

—Julia Child

NO MATTER HOW YOU SPELL IT!

"Stressed spelled backwards is desserts. Coincidence? I think not!"

—Unknown

EGGS BENEDICT, ANYONE?

"If you can master a perfect hollandaise [sauce] you are well on your way to becoming a skilled chef."

—Clara Paul and Eric Trevillé

AGE IS JUST
A NUMBER

"[Bachelors'] approach to gastronomy is basically sexual, since few of them under seventy-nine will bother to produce a good meal unless it is for a pretty woman."

—M.F.K. Fisher

REMAIN CALM IN ANY PIE CRISIS!

"So the pie isn't perfect?
Cut it into wedges. Stay in
control, and never panic."

—Martha Stewart

TECHNIQUE RULES!

"If you learn a recipe, you can cook the recipe. If you learn the technique, you can cook anything."

—Michael Symon

SAVE MONEY, HELP YOUR FAMILY

"Chances are, the food you prepare for your family is going to be far healthier than anything they can order off a menu. Committing to making most of the food your family eats is, in our opinion, the biggest step you can take toward overall nutrition."

—Laura Keogh
and Ceri Marsh
*Creators of
sweetpotatochronicles.com
and authors of
How to Feed a Family*

GO TO A FARMERS' MARKET

"You don't have to cook fancy or complicated masterpieces, just good food from fresh ingredients."

—Julia Child

HASTE MAKES WASTE!

"I always tell my employees, the busier it gets, the slower you should cook. When you run around like a crazy person, that's when things go wrong."

—Michael Symon

NOT IN THE MOOD? GET YOUR PHONE

"If you're not in a good mood, the only thing you should make is a reservation."

—Carla Hall
Chef and television personality

IT'S ABOUT THE WHO AND WHERE...NOT JUST THE WHAT

"To me, food is as much about the moment, the occasion, the location and the company as it is about the taste."

—Heston Blumenthal
British celebrity chef

FIND YOUR
HAPPY PLACE

"Life's too short to settle
for a sad sandwich."

—Haley and Lauren Fox
Restaurateurs

IT'S ALL YOU KNEAD...

"Your hands and a hot oven are the only essential pieces of equipment to bake a loaf of bread."

—Nancy Silverton
Author of Nancy Silverton's
Breads from the La Brea Bakery

'CAUSE SHE'S THE MAMA...THAT'S WHY

"I used to sit in the kitchen and watch my mother and grandmother. By the time I left home, I knew how to cook."

—Jack Schatz
Professional trombonist

WHAT'S IN A NAME?

"You can call it sautéing if it makes you feel better—but it's really just educated frying."

—Stephen King

LOVE, LOVE, LOVE...

"You are the butter to my bread and the breath to my life."

—Julia Child

IT'S ABOUT THE
TIME YOU HAVE

"Fortunately, there is a recipe for cooking. Unwritten, perhaps, and not a recipe for a single dish, but for cooking itself. The ingredient list includes the foodstuffs and equipment available, your skill level, budget, and friends to help clean up, but also—specially—the amount of time you're able to put in."

—Cal Peternell

SCENT SENSE

"The smell of good bread baking, like the sound of lightly flowing water, is indescribable in its evocation of innocence and delight."

—M.F.K Fisher

DIG DEEP

"If you ever find yourself longing to cook a good vegetable but there is none in sight, get a deep pot and dig eight to ten plain, big dusty onions from your pantry, or the cold, dark onion bin at your nearest store.
Then caramelize them."

—Tamar Adler

LIGHTEN UP!

"The important thing, I believe, is to have a really good time cooking. Don't be serious, and—most of all— don't be 'precious.'"

—Linda McCartney

SCIENCE...
IT'S EXACTING

"The biggest challenge of being a pastry chef is that, unlike other types of chefs, you can't throw things together at a farmer's market. When you're working with baking powder and a formula, you have to be exact. If not, things can go wrong."

—Carla Hall

NATURAL TALENT

"Some of the greatest chefs in the world aren't classically trained. Thomas Keller—probably the greatest American chef ever to walk the earth—never went to culinary school."

—Michael Symon

POSITIVELY RICH!

"Having a rich quality of life can be as accessible as a simple supper and a positive state of mind."

—Rachael Ray
TV personality

WRITE YOUR OWN STORY

"Everyone has a story and a recipe. We cherish them because they are our reinventions. Our recipes convey who we were, are, and want to be."

—Edward Lee
Author of
Smoke and Pickles

THERE ARE NO MISTAKES!

"Make mistakes. Over salt, use too much vinegar, make something too spicy, burn something—and then don't do it again. That is how you learn."

—Joshua McFadden
Author of Six Seasons

FOOD LOVE—IT'S REAL

"The phrase 'food is love' has always struck me as a bit sappy and overplayed...but then again, I firmly believe it to be true."

—Katie Workman

TURN UP THE HEAT!

"I'm actually—strongly and earnestly—recommending you make sex a part of the routine of cooking."

—Michael Ruthlman
Author

HEIGHTEN
YOUR SENSES

"Anyone who enjoys cooking develops a sense of what will work."

—Henry Schenck
College professor

IT IS ALL ABOUT HAVING FUN...

"Learn how to cook—
try new recipes, learn from
your mistakes, be fearless
and above all have fun."

—Julia Child

SPICE UP YOUR LIFE

"If you want things to taste right, you need salt."

—Adam Bonin
Lawyer

HEALTHY EATING FOR THE WIN!

"Getting kids to cook is a win-win. They learn how to whip up something good to eat (an important skill that will come in handy throughout their lives). And they're more likely to eat healthy, too."

—Deanna F. Cook

REINVENT THE CHICKEN!

"With a little invention, a simple roast chicken—one of the great staples of cooking life—becomes something entirely new."

—Michael Ruthlman

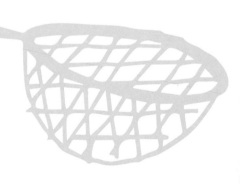

WHY ASK WHY?

"Life is so short; why would one not eat well or bring others to the pleasure of your table?"

—Jim Harrison

EAT THE COOKIE!!

"Don't take it too seriously. Enjoy yourself. That's the deal with grilling and barbecue. Friends and family; laughter and good times. It's not like being at those trendy downtown bars, where everyone is dressed in black and they all look like they need a cookie."

—Al Roker
American television personality and weatherman

"Frying gets a bad name because people get enthusiastic and fry the sh*t out of stuff. The grease splatters; the smoke billows; the smoke detectors go off. No, no, no. Show a little patience. Engage in culinary foreplay."

—Stephen King

BE A REAL MAN...

"If you're a man who abhors sexism, take up the spatula."

—Shankar Vedantam
Author and podcaster

IN THE NICK OF TIME

"In baking, as in many other things, timing is of the essence...Start with a clean kitchen and have everything prepped to go. Once you are organized and have your tools ready, you will have the confidence to mix and bake like a pro."

—Cheryl and Griffith Day
The Back in the Day Bakery Cookbook

SOMEBODY HAS TO FEED THOSE KIDS

"Parenthood and the necessities of daily life taught me, as they have billions others, to cook."

—Mark Bittman
Cookbook author and columnist

LEFTOVERS ARE FOOD, TOO...

"Today's soup is tomorrow's puree."

—Tamar Adler

...AND FOOD WASTE SHOULD BE A CRIME

"The amount of food you have left over from a meal is always the perfect amount for something."

—Tamar Adler

INSTANT GRATIFICATION!

"Cooking is like building a house. It's a manual process. But unlike a house, which might take months to build, cooking takes one night, and that gives me a great sense of satisfaction."

—Josh Lomask
Firefighter

BE SWEET!

"If a man bakes a pie, or a cake, or cupcakes, or cookies, even, he becomes a curiosity to the opposite sex."

—Manuel Gonzalez
Writer

ER: EMERGENCY RIGATONI

"The first thing you need to do when you get home at night is to boil a big pot of water—then you're ready for pasta, or for emergencies that require sterile surgical instruments."

—Sean Wilsey
Writer

IT IS CHILD'S PLAY!

"Many happy childhood memories begin in the kitchen, baking cookies or decorating birthday cakes. It's one of the sweetest parts of childhood."

—Deanna F. Cook

CHOP CHOP!

"If you take 15 minutes or so to prep your week you will be thanking yourself in the days to come: mince some garlic, and some parsley, chop some onions, zest and juice a couple of lemons, just get any ingredients you know you use frequently ready to roll. Tuck them into little containers in the fridge and you'll be good to go when you are ready to get dinner fired up."

—Katie Workman

IT'S ALL IN
THE TIMING

"The foundation of my style
of cooking, which is really
about the same as that of my
grandmother, and probably
your grandmother too:
spend a little time each day
shopping, spend time with
other chores, and then, when
the day is winding down,
figure out dinner."

—Mark Bittman

IT'S A
LOVE-HATE THING...

"You can cook stuff people love to eat without loving to cook."

—Stephen King

SOUS-CHEF DREAMS

"My fantasy meal is not about the ingredients. It's about the prep and the cleanup. Having the prep and the cleanup done for me, that's my fantasy."

—Henry Schenck

MAYBE A TASTEFUL ACCIDENT?

"There are no accidents or miracles, just hard work accompanied by taste."

—Jim Harrison

ALL IT TAKES IS TIME AND PRACTICE

"The more time kids spend in the kitchen experimenting with fresh ingredients and trying out simple kitchen tools, the better they will get at cooking, too. It's like playing soccer or the piano. It takes time and effort to learn to cook, but practice makes perfect."

—Deanna F. Cook

GRILLING GOALS

"I maintain there isn't anything you can't make better by grilling it."

—Al Roker

PARENTING GOALS

"Cooking, along with child rearing, gave me a sense of competence that I'd never had before."

—Mark Bittman

USE YOUR IMAGINATION

"Cooking is both simpler and more necessary than we imagine."

—Tamar Adler

PATIENCE, YOUNG JEDI

"The only thing that stands between you and a tender pork shoulder is time, and patience itself is an important ingredient."

—Julia Turshen

HOORAY FOR
THE COOKS!

"Anyone who cooks
is my hero."

—Violet Lemay
Artist and Illustrator

CRIMES OF FOOD PASSION

"The food you are cooking has, in a sense, already been murdered once; cooking gets easy once you realize that your only responsibility is to not murder it again."

—Tom Junod
American journalist

NO-NO

"There are two things you should never do with your father: learn how to drive and learn how to kill a chicken."

—Gabrielle Hamilton
Chef, author, and restaurateur

LIVE LIFE TO THE FULLEST!

"When I create what I want to eat, the simple task becomes the seed that empowers me to live the life I want, and to create that too. And when I cook and eat in a way that reflects how I want to live, it means I have the opportunity three (or more!) times a day to make decisions that help me live that life. That's why I cook."

—Alana Chernila

STILL, WEAR AN OVEN MITT

"A meal is cooked by the mind, heart and hands of the cook. Not the pots and pans."

—Tamar Adler

WASTE NOT, WANT NOT

"Nothing should be wasted.
Cooking is built upon a deep
preservative impulse."

—Tamar Adler

I DON'T CARE WHAT YOUR MOTHER SAID, PLAY WITH YOUR FOOD!

"It's ok to play with our food—BE innovative, kick it up with spices, with sauces, with fillings, with toppings. Be imaginative. Go beyond the basics. Have fun."

—Emeril Lagasse

ARE YOU A PROBLEM SOLVER?

"There's a pantry, there's a refrigerator, and there is a mind capable of combining ingredients from both to Make Dinner."

—Mark Bittman

BE FEARLESS!

"Don't be afraid to make substitutions. Don't be afraid to add or subtract. Don't be afraid of anything when cooking. That is perhaps the greatest wisdom I can impart; never be afraid of trying or doing anything in the kitchen!"

—Lidia Matticchio Bastianich

OUI OUI!!

"Mise en place. From the French, 'put in place.' The idea is that all ingredients of a recipe should be diced, sliced and prepped before you start cooking."

—Sara Moulton

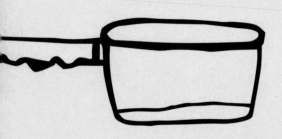

SET YOUR PRIORITIES

"What can be more important than a little something to eat?"

—Winnie the Pooh

POWER DOWN AND FIRE UP!

"Turn off the screens, turn on the oven!"

—Deanna F. Cook

SIZE DOESN'T MATTER.
BUT YOU KNEW THAT.

"The size of your kitchen
should not make or break you."

—Amanda Freitag

SAUTÉ.
DEGLAZE.
REPEAT.

"No one is born a great cook, one learns by doing."

—Julia Child

ONE MEAL AT A TIME

"Becoming a confident cook means mastering one delicious thing at a time, taking pleasure in each small victory."

—Julia Turshen

YOU'VE BEEN WARNED

"Never cook bacon naked."

—Jason Cina
Artist and father

SO MUCH SALAD, SO LITTLE TIME

"Salads are so versatile and easy to make that you could serve a different one every night."

—Sara Moulton

OLIVE OIL HAS SUPERPOWERS

"I challenge anyone to find me a situation a good olive oil can't fix."

—Tamar Adler

BE HAPPY

"Happiness: a good bank account, a good cook, and a good digestion."

—Jean-Jacques Rousseau
French philosopher

SPICE IT UP!

"All ingredients need salt."

—Tamar Adler

IT'S A FAMILY AFFAIR!

"Everybody likes fresh pasta, but people believe it is difficult to make. Today, with a food processor and a small hand pasta-roller, it is a cinch, as well as a great project for the whole family, no matter what age."

—Lidia Matticchio Bastianich

LOVE ALL AROUND

"I don't believe you can ever really cook unless you love eating."

—Nigella Lawson
English journalist and food writer

ZZZZZZZZZZZ

"Most of us tend to make the same 10 recipes over and over again. This is boring, and when you're bored, you're disinclined to make any dinner at all."

—Sara Moulton

JUST DO IT

"In order to become a
baker, I'd have to stop
looking for answers and
just bake some bread."

—Nancy Silverton

THINK OF
THE REWARDS

"The only thing I like better
than talking about food
is eating."

—John Waters
*American filmmaker
and author*

INDEX